KUNG FU

NEIL MORRIS

Heinemann
LIBRARY

www.heinemann.co.uk/library
Visit our website to find out more information about **Heinemann Library** books.

To order:
☎ Phone 44 (0) 1865 888066
▤ Send a fax to 44 (0) 1865 314091
▭ Visit the Heinemann Bookshop at www.heinemann.co.uk/library to browse our catalogue and order online.

First published in Great Britain by Heinemann Library, Halley Court, Jordan Hill, Oxford OX2 8EJ,a division of Reed Educational and Professional Publishing Ltd.
Heinemann is a registered trademark of Reed Educational & Professional Publishing Limited.

OXFORD MELBOURNE AUCKLAND JOHANNESBURG BLANTYRE
GABORONE IBADAN PORTSMOUTH NH (USA) CHICAGO

Designed by Ken Vail Graphic Design, Cambridge
Originated by Dot Gradations
Printed by Wing King Tong in Hong Kong.

ISBN 0 431 11043 3 (hardback)
06 05 04 03 02
10 9 8 7 6 5 4 3 2

ISBN 0 431 11048 4 (paperback)
06 05 04 03 02
10 9 8 7 6 5 4 3 2 1

British Library Cataloguing in Publication Data

Morris, Neil, 1946-
    Kung fu. – (Get Going! Martial arts)
    1.Kung fu – Juvenile literature
    I. Title
    796.8'159

Acknowledgements
The Publishers would like to thank the following for permission to reproduce photographs: Corbis, p.12; Simon T. Lailey p.7(b); Rex Features, p.7(t); Rex Features/Kuan Cheng/Xinhua, p.5; Ronald Grant Archive, p.29; All other photographs by Trevor Clifford.

Cover photograph reproduced with permission of Earl and Nazima Kowall/Corbis.

Our thanks to Sandra Beale, Director of Coaching and Administration, National Association of Karate and Martial Art Schools, for her comments in the preparation of this book. Our thanks also to James Sinclair of the UK Wing Chun Association, as well as to Ben, Anthony, Anna, Naomi, Sam, Joseph, Niah and Sheridan, for their help with the photographs.

Every effort has been made to contact copyright holders of any material reproduced in this book. Any omissions will be rectified in subsequent printings if notice is given to the Publisher.

Words appearing in the text in bold, **like this**, are explained in the Glossary.

CONTENTS

! Do remember that martial arts need to be taught by a qualified, registered instructor, or teacher. Don't try any of the techniques and movements in this book without such an instructor present.

WHAT IS KUNG FU?

Kung fu is a general term used for all Chinese martial arts. Since the People's Republic of China has the largest population of any country in the world – at least 1.2 billion people, or about a fifth of the world's population – it is not surprising that there are hundreds of different forms of kung fu. The term is not easy to translate, but perhaps the closest equivalent is 'skill expert'. The Chinese word for 'martial art' is *wushu*, a term that is also sometimes used to cover all the different Chinese arts, in a similar way to kung fu. Some people use kung fu when they mean the exercise and self-defence aspects of the martial art, and wushu for the competitive sport.

All over the country there are many kung fu clubs with experienced teachers.

NORTHERN FOOT, SOUTHERN FIST

The many different schools of kung fu are traditionally divided into styles that came originally from northern and southern China. There is a phrase 'northern foot, southern fist', which means that the northern styles contain a lot of kicking **techniques**, whereas the southern styles are based more on use of the hands. Northern styles have a great deal of movement, and may well have developed their leg techniques in ancient times when many opponents were mounted horsemen. Southern styles include more close-quarter techniques, and some are so specialist that they are still named after the family names of their founders, such as *hung gar*, *lau gar* and *mok gar* (*gar* means family).

WHERE TO LEARN AND PRACTISE

This book tells you how to set about starting kung fu. It also shows and explains some kung fu techniques, so that you can understand and practise them. But you must always remember that you cannot learn any martial art just from a book. To take up and study kung fu seriously you must go to regular lessons with a qualified teacher, so that you learn all the techniques properly and then repeat and practise them many times.

YOUR KUNG FU CLUB

Choose your club carefully. It should have an experienced teacher and it should belong to a martial arts association. The list on page 31 gives the names and addresses of organizations that can give you national and local information, as well as lists of clubs.

These students are giving an outdoor demonstration of kung fu.

KUNG FU THROUGH HISTORY

All the world's martial arts can be traced back to Ancient China, which had a strong influence on Korea, Japan and the rest of the Far East. Chinese clans, families and individuals learned to defend themselves during many troubled periods in ancient times. About 2500 years ago, there were battles between huge armies with horse-drawn chariots, bronze swords and deadly crossbows. The Chinese armies had a total of more than six million soldiers, and in one battle in 260 BC half a million men were killed. The land was also full of bandits, which encouraged young men to learn to defend themselves and their families.

This map shows Korea, Japan and China.

Around 1500 years ago, a famous monastery and temple were founded in the mountains of Henan province, in central China. In order to protect their temple – called Shaolin – against bandits, the monks trained hard to become fit and strong. Around AD 520, an Indian monk called Bodhidharma came to the Shaolin Temple. He taught a form of **meditation** known as

Zen Buddhism (or *Chan* in Chinese). The Shaolin Temple became a leading martial arts school, combining skills of self-defence with a peaceful way of life.

Over a thousand years later, in 1674, a fire destroyed the temple. Some say it was started by a monk on behalf of the emperor, who feared it was becoming too powerful.

These life-sized warrior figures were buried in 210 BC near the tomb of the Chinese Emperor.

According to legend, just five monks and a nun survived the fire, and they became the founders of modern martial arts.

WING CHUN

The nun who survived the Shaolin fire, Ng Mui, was a martial arts expert. Moving to the south of China, she met a young woman named Yim Wing Chun, whom she taught. When the young woman asked her teacher what the martial art was called, Ng Mui named it after her pupil – Wing Chun, which means 'humming in springtime'. At the time Wing Chun was being bothered by a bully who wanted to marry her. Her father cleverly told the bully that his daughter would only marry someone who could beat her in a fight. Wing Chun easily defended herself against the bully and the rest of his gang, which left her free to marry the young man she loved. Today, her style of kung fu, known as *wing chun*, is one of the best known throughout the world. Many of the **techniques** in this book are based on this style.

A Shaolin temple in China today.

IN THE KWOON

Kung fu is practised and performed in a casual training outfit, which is traditionally black. It is best to buy a suit through your club, but you don't need one immediately. For the first few sessions, a tracksuit or T-shirt and training bottoms will probably do, but check this with the club first. When you do buy your kung fu suit, make sure that it is large enough so that your movements are not restricted in any way.

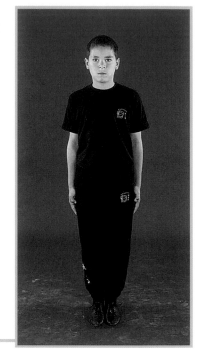

It is important to treat your outfit with respect. Always keep it clean. Wash and iron it regularly, and fold it carefully after each training session. A neat and tidy appearance shows that you have the right attitude to training. Inside the training hall or gymnasium, called a *kwoon*, you should wear special, lightweight kung fu shoes. For the first few sessions trainers will do.

A Kung fu suit.

! SAFETY

In order not to harm yourself or anyone else, don't wear a watch or any jewellery. Keep your fingernails and toenails trimmed short. Tie long hair back, but never with metal clips.

Make sure that you are fit enough to be very active, and don't train if you are ill. Exercise should not hurt, so never push yourself to the point where you feel pain. Tell your instructor if you suffer from any medical condition.

Groin protectors are a good idea for boys, and boys and girls should wear mouthguards in any form of competition.

All martial arts can be dangerous if they are not performed properly. Never fool around inside or outside the training hall – or at home or in school – by showing off or pretending to have a real fight.

COURTESY

It is important for any martial arts student to show respect to everyone and everything to do with their sport. As a sign of respect, there are several formal kung fu greetings. They vary in different schools. This is a wing chun greeting.

1 Stand with your feet together and your arms at your sides.

2 Make a fist with one hand and place it in the palm of your other hand, in front of you at chin level. Make sure that your face is friendly and not **aggressive**.

WOODEN DUMMY

Some kung fu schools use a wooden dummy, which is designed to act as a replica of the human body. Kung fu artists use it to practise and develop their striking and **blocking techniques**.

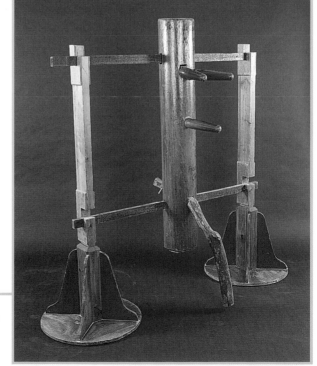

The Chinese name for the training dummy is mook yan jong.

WARMING UP

Kung fu gives you a lot of hard, physical exercise. It is important to warm your body up and stretch your muscles before training, so that you don't injure yourself. At your club you will always start a session with some warm-up exercises. You might begin by walking or jogging on the spot for a couple of minutes, before doing some stretching exercises.

IMPORTANT

- Never exercise too hard when it is very hot or humid. Normally, the cool, dry kwoon ensures that this is not the case.

- Never exercise or practise kung fu when you are ill or injured.

- Try not to breathe too hard and fast when you are exercising or resting.

- Don't hold your breath while you are exercising or practising kung fu.

- When you are stretching, you should always remain comfortable and your muscles should not hurt. If you feel pain, stop at once.

- Begin your kung fu exercises immediately after warming up.

ARM CIRCLES

1 Stand up straight with your feet a shoulder-width apart.

2 Stretch your arms out to the sides at shoulder level and then take them around in forward circles. Do ten circles, making them as large as you can.

3 Repeat the ten circles, this time backwards.

UPPER BACK STRETCH

1 Stand up straight and clasp your hands together behind your back, intertwining your fingers.

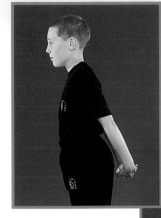

2 Lift your hands up as high as you can and as far away from your back as possible. Hold this position for a count of five and then return to the starting position.

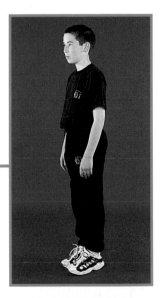

3 Repeat the exercise five times.

QUADRICEPS STRETCH

The quadriceps are the large muscles at the front of your thighs.

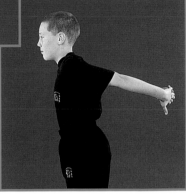

1 Stand up straight, with your feet a shoulder width apart.

2 Raise your left knee and take hold of your left ankle with your left hand.

3 Take your left leg back until your heel is close to your bottom.

4 Hold this position for a count of ten, keeping your knees close together.

5 Repeat the exercise with the other leg.

(For cooling down exercises see page 25.)

STYLES AND FORMS

ANIMAL MOVEMENTS

Many of the hundreds of different kung fu styles developed in ancient times from people carefully watching and copying the movements of animals. The tiger, leopard, dragon, crane and snake are the most famous animal styles. The tiger and leopard styles use slashing strikes, developed from the strong claws of the big wild cats, and the dragon style is very powerful.

The crane style of kung fu came from copying the bird's movements.

The crane and the snake are less **aggressive** styles, and are the basis for much of the famous wing chun style of kung fu. Many of the **techniques** in this book are based on wing chun.

The crane style.

The crane is a tall, long-legged bird that appears in many Chinese legends. In the crane style, the martial artist makes her thumb and fingers into a beak shape. She pecks at her opponent with her two hand-beaks.

The 'snake' usually coils up and then suddenly springs at her opponent, striking with her fingertips.

The snake style.

PATTERNS

Kung fu styles have their own forms, or **patterns**. These are made up of a series of set moves that are practised to improve technique and help an artist learn about attack, defence and **counter-attack**. The moves are like training drills with an imaginary opponent. As you learn the forms, your instructor (*sifu* in Chinese) will constantly check that your technique is correct.

The patterns all start from a basic training position. Make relaxed fists and pull them up to the sides of your chest. Stand with your legs a shoulder width apart and bend your knees slightly.

The basic training position.

Opening hand – side view.

HAND POSITIONS

In the wing chun style, several basic hand positions are used and practised throughout the forms. At the same time, these hand positions help make the wrists stronger and more flexible.

To make the opening hand (called *tan sau* in Chinese), open your left hand and very slowly move it forwards until your elbow is in front of your chest. Your right hand should be in the middle of your body.

Opening hand.

PUNCHING

Kung fu punches are famous for being very powerful. The wing chun basic punch, in particular, develops a lot of power, even though it often travels a very short distance. You can practise punching without an opponent. When you have learned the basic skills, you may be allowed to practise against an opponent holding a **focus pad**.

The power of the punch comes at the very last moment, so a powerful blow can be made over just a few centimetres. Timing is vital, and you must learn to focus your energy at the right moment, or the energy is wasted.

WING CHUN PUNCH

1 Start from the basic training position (see page 13). Open one hand as you put it forward and point your fingers at the imaginary target.

2 As you start to make a punch by straightening your elbow, close your fingers to make a fist. Put your thumb on top of your fist as you clench your fingers tightly.

3 Hit the target with the lower three knuckles, focusing all your energy into your fist and keeping your thumb on top. Make sure that your arm stays slightly bent when you punch, so as not to put too much strain on your elbow.

There is a special version of this move called the one-inch punch (*chun ging*), which is very short and extremely powerful.

THE CENTRE LINE

Many kung fu punches are aimed at the centre of the opponent's body. There is an imaginary centre line running from the top of the head and down the middle of the face and body.

From this all-important centre line, you can divide the body into **zones** and **gates**. There are three basic zones: the high zone, from the top of the head to the chest; the middle zone, from the solar plexus (or pit of the stomach) to the groin; and the low zone, from the hips to the toes. Each of the zones has an inner and an outer gate, which lie either side of the centre line.

In wing chun kung fu, students are trained to use the right **block** and **counter-attack** depending on which zone is attacked. At the same time, the blocks will try to open up the opponent's centre line.

STRIKING

Strikes are like punches, but they use other parts of the hand and arm instead of the closed fist. They are practised without an opponent or as part of a training drill. Later you may be allowed to try some of the moves in **sparring** sessions with a partner, which give you the opportunity to test the skills you have learned and practised. At first, all the sparring will be pre-arranged, which means that both partners agree beforehand what they are going to do. This makes it easier for both partners to learn how to use combinations properly and get their timing right.

THRUSTING FINGERS

This powerful strike comes originally from the snake style of kung fu and uses strong fingers to attack an opponent's eyes. As in the basic punch, all the striker's energy should be put into their fingers at the very last moment.

 SPARRING SAFETY

When sparring or just practising a strike, you must concentrate very hard and make sure that you do not actually hit your partner. Always work with your partner, so that you help each other and learn together. The balance you learned during all the hours of practice without a partner will help you. At the same time, you must remember to look after yourself, too. Always keep your guard up, and take special care with your own head as well as your partner's.

KNIFE HAND

The knife hand is similar to the '**karate** chop' that a lot of people associate with karate. The target is hit with the little-finger edge of the hand.

PALM-HEEL STRIKE

This sort of strike is particularly useful if your opponent is moving forwards, so that he walks into it and increases its force. It is particularly effective when aimed at the chin or jaw.

ELBOW STRIKE

This is a powerful short-range strike that thrusts the point of the elbow into the opponent's jaw, chin or ribs. In this case, the student has also taken the opportunity to grab his opponent's wrist. This particular move (grabbing hand, or *lap sau*) is used a great deal in kung fu, to keep your opponent where you want them to be.

KICKING

Kung fu kicks are powerful weapons. They have a greater reach than punches or other strikes, but because they have to travel a long way to hit their target, an opponent has more time to avoid them. Most kung fu kicks begin with the leg bent at the knee. The leg is then straightened to hit the target with the foot, but never with the toes. It is important to keep the leg slightly bent, so as not to put too much strain on the knee.

The northern Chinese kung fu styles have high, spectacular kicks. In the southern styles, such as wing chun, the kicks are lower and tend to be aimed at the opponent's ankles, shins or knees.

FRONT KICK

You will probably learn this kick first, since it is the most basic kicking **technique**. From the basic training position, bend your knees and keep your right fist up to guard your face. Bring your left leg forward and raise your left foot, pulling the toes back.

When your left knee is high, thrust out your left leg, pushing your hips into the kick. Imagine that you are hitting the target (your opponent's stomach) with your heel. Keep your guard up during the kick.

SIDE KICK

For this kick you start sideways-on to your opponent. This beginning position is often called a cat **stance**. Raise your right foot and drive your heel downwards. In a real situation, this would hit your opponent's knee.

HOOK KICK

This self-defence technique is a basic move in the form of kung fu developed by martial arts expert and film star Bruce Lee (see page 28). It is unusual because you do not lift your knee, you just give a circular kick straight from the hip.

BLOCKING

In any martial art, players have to learn to defend themselves against attacks by their opponent. Even the best attacking martial artists also need good defending **technique**. Many of the basic moves in kung fu start with a **block**, used to fend off an attack by the opponent. This acts as a good reminder that the true spirit of all martial arts is never to strike the first blow but to defend against **aggression**. A good block will upset the opponent's balance and force them into a position where they are open to a **counter-attack**.

 ## SAFETY FIRST

Remember that you must only practise blocking moves at your martial arts club, where they will be properly supervised. If you are pretending to hit your opponent, aim to fall well short of your target. Every martial artist must be responsible for the safety of their partner as well as themselves.

Two basic blocks use either side of the blocking arm to turn an opponent's punch away from or across the body.

FIRST BLOCK

As the opponent comes in with a punch, raise your right hand, palm side upwards. Deflect the opponent's punch with the thumb side of your hand and arm. This will divert the strike across your opponent's body so that he or she cannot now reach you with either fist.

SECOND BLOCK

1 This time, as your opponent comes in with a punch you again raise your right hand, palm side upwards.

2 Now deflect your opponent's punch with the little finger side of your hand and arm. This diverts his or her strike across your body. You can even take the opportunity to turn the blocking hand into a fist and punch your opponent.

RELAXATION AND ENERGY

Chinese martial artists strongly believe in relaxing both the mind and the body. One way to do this is by breathing correctly. Instead of just using the upper part of the chest to breathe, use the lower chest and diaphragm (the large sheet of muscle below the lungs that plays an important part in our breathing). Good breathing helps relaxation, and Chinese martial artists believe that this produces *qi*, or energy. They believe that qi is stored in an area called the *dantien*, a spot just below the navel which is the body's centre of gravity.

STICKING HANDS

A lot of kung fu involves close-range **sparring** between two partners. This means that attacks can come very quickly one after the other. Artists have to learn to recognize the moves that are coming and deal with them correctly and fast.

Sticking hands (or *chi sau*) is a special form of training for close combat that is unique to kung fu. It teaches you how to deal with all the pushing, grabbing and grappling that go on. You practise getting in close to your partner, blocking their moves and **counter-attacking** with your own.

In order to develop the skills of sticking hands, you need to go to regular kung fu classes and learn from a good teacher. You work in pairs, and both partners can learn the basics of close fighting skills without hurting each other. Beginners start with single sticking hands and eventually move on to the double form of training.

These starting sequences give an idea of the two forms.

SINGLE HAND

1 The student on the right makes the opening hand we saw earlier, which is also a palm-up **block**. The student on the left rests his wrist on Right's arm in a so-called resting hand position.

2 Right turns his hand and attacks with a palm strike, which Left blocks by forcing it down with a so-called sinking hand.

3 Left turns the block into an attack by punching towards Right. Right uses a wing-arm block by raising his right arm, but keeping his wrist relaxed.

4 The two partners return to the first position and go through the sequence again and again.

DOUBLE HANDS

1 The student on the right rests his right arm on the outside of Left's arm. Left has his right arm on the outside of Right's arm.

2 Both partners roll their hands up and down, changing their hand positions but constantly keeping in contact. When you get used to this, you will start to feel what your partner is going to do next.

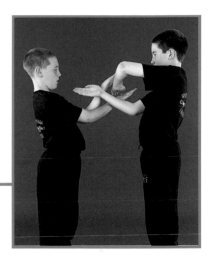

3 The boy on the right pushes his right arm to the ouside of Left's arm. This is called changing **gates**.

4 Right now pushes his right arm through, grabs left's neck (making sure that he does not hurt him) and pulls his head forwards. Left's arms are trapped, so Right can choose the next movement.

5 This sequence could go on in different ways, and then be repeated.

SELF-DEFENCE

Many people take up a martial art in order to learn self-defence. They want to learn **techniques** that will be useful if they are unfortunate enough to need them. The various schools of kung fu all have different approaches to self-defence, but most of their moves lend themselves naturally to this use.

Learning kung fu skills builds up your self-confidence, especially if you are shy by nature. Others will see that you are confident – that is, happy with yourself, rather than a show-off – and you are less likely to be seen as a target by any potential bully. Many kung fu moves are based on using a small amount of energy to defeat much greater force. This means that a small, calm person can overcome a larger, **aggressive** opponent.

FOCUS PADS

Remember, when you punch in a **sparring** session, your fist must fall just short of your opponent so that he or she is not actually touched. You may wear special fist mitts in case you accidentally do strike your opponent. You can practise punching by having a partner hold up one or two **focus pads**. Punching against pads will give you confidence to hit hard. The pads can also be used for practising kicks and other strikes.

PROFESSIONAL PRACTICE

Kung fu can be an excellent way to defend yourself. But remember: you must only practise self-defence moves with your instructor present, so that you are shown the correct way to do them. You don't want to get hurt practising self-defence!

Using any martial art in self-defence is a last resort. If someone is bothering you, it is always best to tell them first that you don't want a fight. If possible, find help as quickly as you can. Tell a teacher, your parents or any grown-up you trust. Always avoid a fight, but never keep problems to yourself.

! COOLING DOWN

It is important to cool down gently after energetic exercise such as kung fu. You can do this by jogging or walking, deep breathing and by doing some gentle stretching exercises. These could be the same as you did when you warmed up (see pages 10–11).

Or you could do some other stretches. For example windmills are similar to arm circles, except that you swing one arm at a time. Some students like to cool down by doing some **patterns** to music.

Arm circles

Back stretch

Quadriceps stretch.

TAI CHI

If you have heard of *tai chi*, you probably think of it as a system of Chinese exercises. It is true that in the parks and open spaces of modern China, especially early in the morning, you see people going through tai chi movements. Many tai chi students are older, retired people, and these routines are very good for their health.

Tai chi chuan, to use the full name, is in fact a martial art. It is a form of kung fu, and its name means 'great ultimate boxing'. According to tradition, it was first developed by a 13th-century priest named Chang San Feng, who studied at the Shaolin Temple. He was a **Taoist** who was supposedly influenced in his development of the art by watching the fluid movements of a snake and a stork as they fought. Tai chi is still strongly linked to Taoist beliefs.

THE HOOK

This example of a tai chi movement and position is known as *tan pien*, or the hook.

1 Put your left leg forward and put your weight on it. Hold your left hand in front of you. Hold your right hand behind you, curling your fingers and thumb into a hook position.

2 Slowly and smoothly turn your right foot outwards and begin to move your weight onto the back foot. At the same time begin to lower your left hand (this is actually a **block** against a striking **technique**).

3 Bend your right leg until it forms a right angle. Slide your left arm down your left leg, keeping your back straight. Throughout the exercise you should keep your eyes looking forward at an imaginary opponent.

YIN AND YANG

All Chinese martial arts are linked to religious or **philosophical** beliefs. Many are related to the Taoist beliefs of yin and yang. Taoists follow the teachings of Lao-tzu, who lived in the 6th century BC and believed that people should live simple lives in tune with nature. In the symbol of yin and yang,

the dark and the light are clasped together and each contains a tiny amount of the other. The yin is dark, cool, feminine and soft; the yang is light, hot, masculine and hard. Some kung fu schools are said to be 'hard', while others are 'soft'.

ALL AROUND THE WORLD

Kung fu has grown and spread from China throughout the world. At the same time it has kept its many different schools and approaches, which makes it complicated as a world sport. The International Wushu Federation based in Beijing in China organizes world championships which have six different events. There are separate sections for men and women. Many of them use traditional Chinese weapons. The events include a northern style with jumps and footwork, a southern style with hand movements, tai chi, and fighting with a **broadsword**, **cudgel** and spear.

GRADING

Unlike Japanese and Korean martial arts, kung fu does not have an official form of grading to show students how they are progressing. However, some schools use a series of coloured sashes, such as this:

sash colour		grade
yellow	≈	1st (beginner)
orange	≈	2nd
green	≈	3rd
blue	≈	4th
brown	≈	5th
black	≈	1st to 10th degree (expert)

BRUCE LEE

Many people around the world would never have heard of kung fu if it had not been for Bruce Lee. Born Lee Yuan Kam in San Francisco in 1940, Bruce spent most of his childhood in Hong Kong, where he learned kung fu. He studied **philosophy** at the University of Washington and during the 1960s he started acting on television. His big break came in 1971, when he returned to Hong Kong to make a martial arts film called *Fists of Fury*. In 1973 he made *Enter the Dragon*, which is considered to be the best kung fu movie.

Bruce Lee was a student of Ip Man, a **grand master** in wing chun. He also developed his own form of kung fu, called *jeet kune do* ('the way of the intercepting fist') or JKD. He always insisted, however, that this was not a new style and that his aim was to free martial artists from clinging to specific styles or methods. In the 1970s, Bruce Lee's films, which are full of action and amazing fight sequences, were so popular that they increased the world's awareness of kung fu, **karate** and the martial arts in general.

In 1973, during the filming of *Game of Death*, Bruce Lee died suddenly at the age of 32. His son Brandon (1965–93) became an action film star, but also died at a young age.

Film star Bruce Lee in action in the film, Enter the Dragon.

CHINESE WORDS

Chinese words	Meaning	Chinese words	Meaning
chi sau	sticking hands	*mook yan jong*	training dummy
chun ging	one-inch punch	*qi*	energy
dantien	spot just below the navel (the body's centre of gravity)	*sifu*	instructor
		tai chi chuan	'great ultimate boxing', a martial art
gar	family		
jeet kune do	'way of intercepting a fist', a form of kung fu developed by Bruce Lee	*tan pien*	hook
		tan sau	opening hand position
		wing chun	a style of kung fu, meaning 'humming in springtime'
kwoon	training hall		
lap sau	grabbing hand move	*wushu*	martial art

GLOSSARY

aggressive quarrelsome, hostile behaviour

block to stop an opponent's attack

broadsword sword with a wide blade

counter-attack attack that replies to an attack by an opponent

cudgel thick stick used as a weapon

focus pad pad or padded glove that can be held up by a partner so that you can practise punching and kicking against it

gate area of attack and defence that covers certain parts of the body

grand master expert of the highest class

karate Japanese martial art that uses hands and feet to make high-energy punches, strikes and kicks

meditation exercising the mind by thinking, especially about religion

pattern set of moves that is learned as a training drill

philosophy set of beliefs, often designed to help people be good or become wise

sparring practice contest between two martial arts sudents, sometimes with the moves agreed in advance

stance position of the body, with the feet in a special place and the arms held in a special way

Taoist following the philosophy of Lao-tzu, who lived in ancient China in the 6th century BC

technique method you learn to perform a particular skill

Zen Buddhism form of the Buddhist religion in which meditation is particularly important

zone area of attack and defence that covers certain parts of the body

BOOKS

Kung Fu by Eddie Ferrie, Crowood, Marlborough, 1994

The Complete Book of Martial Arts by David Mitchell, Reed, London, 1993

The Ultimate Book of Martial Arts by Fay Goodman, Anness, London, 1998

The Young Martial Artist by David Mitchell, Penguin, London, 1992

The Young Martial Arts Enthusiast by David Mitchell, Dorling Kindersley, London, 1997

Top Sport: Martial Arts by Bernie Blackall, Heinemann Library, Oxford, 1998

Wing Chun Traditional Kung Fu by Ip Chun and Michael Tse, Piatkus, London, 1998

USEFUL ADDRESSES

Sport England
16 Upper Woburn Place
London WC1H 0QP
020 7273 1500
www.english.sports.gov.uk

Sport Scotland
Caledonia House
South Gyle
Edinburgh EH12 9DQ
0131 317 7200
www.sportscotland.org.uk

Sport Council for Wales
Sophia Gardens
Cardiff CF1 9SW
029 2030 0500
www.sports-council-wales.co.uk

Sport Council for Northern Ireland
Upper Malone Road
Belfast BT9 5LA
028 9038 1222
www.sportni.org

Martial Arts Development Commission
PO Box 381
Erith DA8 1TF
01322 431440
www.madec.org

UK Martial Arts Federation
9 The Meade
Chorltonville
Manchester M21 8FA
07000 627842

International Wushu Federation
2 Andling Road
Chaoyang District
Beijing 100101, China
1 06491 2153
www.worldsport.com/wushu

British Council for Chinese Martial Arts
31 Neale Drive
Greasby
Wirral
Merseyside CH49 1SL
www.bccma.org.uk

National Association of Karate &
   Martial Art Schools
Rosecraig
Bullockstone Road
Herne Bay CT6 7NL
01227 370055
www.nakmas.org.uk

Liang-I Shaolin Kung Fu
The Telstra Centre
Level 1
242 Exhibition St
Melbourne 3000, Australia
www.ozemail.com.au/~kfmaster/

Australian WingTsun Organisation
PO Box 368
Kensington NSW 1465
Australia
1300 134 480
www.wingtsun.com.au

INDEX